FORENSIC INVESTIGATIONS
OF THE
AZTECS

James Bow

CRABTREE
PUBLISHING COMPANY
WWW.CRABTREEBOOKS.COM

Author: James Bow

Editors: Sarah Eason, John Andrews,
  Petrice Custance, and Janine Deschenes

Proofreader and indexer: Wendy Scavuzzo

Editorial director: Kathy Middleton

Design: Paul Myerscough, Paul Oakley,
  and Jane McKenna

Cover design: Paul Myerscough

Photo research: Rachel Blount

**Production coordinator and
  Prepress technician:** Tammy McGarr

Print coordinator: Katherine Berti

Consultant: John Malam

Produced for Crabtree Publishing Company by
Calcium Creative Ltd.

Photo Credits:
t=Top, c=Center, b=Bottom, l=Left, r=Right.

Inside: Flickr: Dennis Jarvis: p. 17; Shutterstock:
123455543: p. 11b b/g; Andreiuc88: p. 20; Aysa_t: p.
22br; Comaniciu Dan: p. 19; Philip Date: p. 29; Everett
Historical: p. 26; Likoper: p. 6; Antwon McMullen: p.
14; Microgen: p. 25t; Mironmax Studio: p. 13; Chansom
Pantip: p. 27t; Tom Reichner: p. 23; Ilya Royz: p. 9;
THPStock: p. 18; Urfin: p. 27b; Valentyn Volkov: p.
7t; Wikimedia Commons: Rafał Chałgasiewicz (Own
work): p. 15; Gargancio: p. 4; Grooverpedro: p. 24; Hans
Hillewaert: p. 7b; Peter Isotalo: p. 22bl; Adam Jones:
p. 25b; Jschmeling: p. 21b; Thomas Ledl: p. 28; David
Monniaux: p. 19b; Wolfgang Sauber: p. 5; S Shepherd:
p. 19t; The Charles Machine Works: p. 11bl; Ulises.
rubin: p. 10; Christoph Weiditz: p. 8; Z-m-k: pp. 1, 12.

Cover: Left from top to bottom: The Charles Machine
Works; Flickr/Dennis Jarvis; Wikimedia/Thomas Ledl;
Right: Wikimedia Commons/Gryffindor.

Library and Archives Canada Cataloguing in Publication

Bow, James, 1972-, author
    Forensic investigations of the Aztecs / James Bow.

(Forensic footprints of ancient worlds)
Includes index.
Issued in print and electronic formats.
ISBN 978-0-7787-4943-1 (hardcover).--
ISBN 978-0-7787-4956-1 (softcover).--
ISBN 978-1-4271-2116-5 (HTML)

    1. Aztecs--Antiquities--Juvenile literature. 2. Mexico--
Antiquities--Juvenile literature. 3. Forensic archaeology--
Mexico--Juvenile literature. 4. Archaeology and history--
Mexico--Juvenile literature. I. Title.

F1219.73.B68 2018   j972'.01809009   C2018-902983-8
                                             C2018-902984-6

Library of Congress Cataloging-in-Publication Data

CIP available at the Library of Congress

Crabtree Publishing Company

www.crabtreebooks.com   1-800-387-7650

Printed in the U.S.A./092018/CG20180719

Published in Canada
Crabtree Publishing
616 Welland Ave.
St. Catharines, Ontario
L2M 5V6

Published in the United States
Crabtree Publishing
PMB 59051
350 Fifth Avenue, 59th Floor
New York, New York 10118

Published in the United Kingdom
Crabtree Publishing
Maritime House
Basin Road North, Hove
BN41 1WR

Published in Australia
Crabtree Publishing
3 Charles Street
Coburg North
VIC, 3058

CONTENTS

Investigating the Aztecs 4

Solving Past Mysteries 6

Digging Up the Aztecs 8

The Great Temple 10

People of the Past 12

The Tower of Skulls 14

A Bundle of Bones 16

Lost Cities Found! 18

Rivers of Danger 20

A Turkey Dinner? 22

Mummy Mystery 24

End of the Empire 26

Forensic Future 28

Can Forensics Solve...? 29

Glossary 30

Learning More 31

Index and About the Author 32

INVESTIGATING THE AZTECS

Around 800 years ago, a tribe of nomads appeared in the Valley of Mexico. They called themselves the Aztecs after their mythical homeland of Aztlán. The Aztecs had no land of their own and traveled up and down the valley, working where they could to scrape together a living. Eventually, the Aztecs settled on an island in the middle of Lake Texcoco around 1325 c.e.

The Aztecs began to build the city of Tenochtitlan, meaning "place of the prickly pear cactus." They ruled central and southern Mexico for the next 200 years. They built temples in the shape of pyramids and quickly built it into one of the most impressive cities ever built. The landscape of Mexico small cities to great palace with two gods. But who were the Aztecs and what do we know about them?

« Forensic scientists use the latest technology to explore the hidden secrets of great Aztec buildings such as this step pyramid.

These bones and other artifacts were found by archaeologists at an Aztec site in Mexico City. They were part of a burial site containing at least 50 bodies. Forensic tests on the bones and teeth revealed that some of the buried people were children who had been **sacrificed**.

HOW SCIENCE SOLVED THE PAST:
FORENSIC FOOTPRINTS

To solve crimes, forensic scientists examine evidence from the places where crimes took place, which are called **crime scenes**. The **techniques** they use to solve crimes are also used by people to solve mysteries about the past. **Archaeologists** and **anthropologists** study the clues, or forensic footprints, ancient people left behind to find out more about them. Archaeologists use forensic techniques to find out more about ancient buildings and **sites**. Anthropologists use forensic techniques to learn more about ancient peoples from their skeletons and the objects they left behind.

Spanish Invaders

DID You Know?

To please their gods, the Aztecs killed people and animals. These killings are called sacrifices. To find out more about them, forensic scientists examine bones to learn if they belonged to animals or humans. They study the tools used to kill sacrifice victims. These tools might contain centuries-old dried blood in their grooves and cracks. Testing the blood tells scientists if the blood belonged to an animal or a human. Depending on the blood sample, scientists can also tell if it belonged to a male or a female.

SOLVING PAST MYSTERIES

Forensic scientists can help police find a body in a recent crime scene and they can also find out where bodies were buried long ago. They dig up any items buried with the bodies, carefully make a note of them, and **preserve** them. They then use forensic science to find out more about the bodies and items.

Putting Human Pieces Together

Forensic scientists study skeletons or bodies to solve mysteries about a crime, and they also study ancient **remains** to find out who people were. They can carry out tests to find out when and why they died. Using the skulls of the dead, scientists can also use special **scanners** and computers to model their faces.

So, what clues, or forensic footprints, did the Aztecs leave behind and what can we learn from them? Let's follow their forensic footprint trail!

HOW SCIENCE SOLVED THE PAST:

MODELING MYSTERIES

We cannot visit the past, but we can model it. Forensic scientists use clues from ancient sites to figure out how the buildings that once stood there looked. For example, **foundations** in the ground hint at where walls might have been. Areas in which broken pottery is buried hint at garbage sites. Using this information, archaeologists use a computer to create a **three-dimensional (3-D)** model of the site as it might once have been. This helps them learn about how the buildings were made and what they might have been used for.

Scientists can also use clues from the past to make 3-D models of people who lived long ago. They study skulls and skeletons to figure out what a person looked like, and use the information to create a 3-D model of the person.

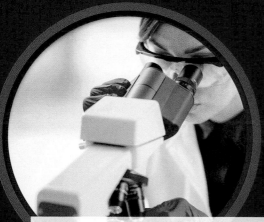

 Forensic scientists use powerful *microscopes* to examine tiny pieces of evidence that cannot be seen by the human eye.

Forensic tests on Aztec artifacts can find tiny traces of cacao beans (shown above), which are used to make chocolate.

 Chemical tests on this mask, made in the shape of two snakes twisting together, showed that the blue **mosaic** pieces were attached using tree **resin**.

DIGGING UP THE AZTECS

The area in which the Aztec **civilization** developed is today called Mexico. Its capital, Mexico City, was built on top of the ruins of the Aztec city of Tenochtitlan. Builders and workmen in Mexico City often find ancient Aztec sites when making repairs or doing building work. In 2010, builders working on a new subway station discovered part of a building. Archaeologists were called in. They dug down farther and found a ball game court!

A Serious Game

Then, the archaeologists found a pile of bones in the court. Forensic experts examined the bones, and decided they were human. The archaeologists started to piece the puzzle together. The Conquistadors described how the Aztecs played a ball game in courts such as the one in Mexico City. Players tried to get a ball through a stone hoop without using their hands or letting the ball touch the ground. This was a game with serious consequences—the unlucky losing team was sometimes sacrificed. Could the bones belong to such a team?

« This picture was drawn by the Spanish around 1530. It shows Aztecs playing their favorite ball game. Pictures and writings help point archaeologists to what they might find using forensics.

Experts can tell a dog skull from other animal skulls by its shape and teeth. A skull can provide many forensic clues about how the Aztecs treated animals.

HOW SCIENCE SOLVED THE PAST:

BLOOD ON THE COURT

Bones can be the result of sacrifice, war, murder, or just a natural death. We can normally tell which of the above was the cause from the place the bones are discovered. However, forensic scientists also test the ground where bones are found to find more clues. When testing soil from the ball game court, scientists discovered chemicals found only in human blood. Marks on the bones also showed that the victims had been deliberately killed.

THE GREAT TEMPLE

Not only did workers digging in Mexico City find the ball game court, they also found a huge stone carving of an Aztec goddess. Experts soon realized that it stood on the site of the Templo Mayor—one of the Aztec's most important religious areas.

Into the Unknown

Archaeologists were excited because within the building they discovered a passageway that could lead to the tomb of an Aztec emperor. To date, no tomb of an Aztec emperor has been found! However, the site is one of the most difficult places to dig. It is very narrow and filled with water, rocks, and mud. Experts have to dig very carefully so they do not damage any artifacts.

DID You Know?

When archaeologists dig up a site, the Sun and air can damage the artifacts. Forensic scientists have many tools to preserve ancient remains and artifacts, and to protect them from the Sun and air. These include special chemicals that can help preserve wood and even paint.

These are just some of the bones and artifacts found at the Templo Mayor. Forensic tests on the objects and human remains will help us learn more about how the Aztecs lived.

HOW SCIENCE SOLVED THE PAST:

SECRETS OF THE HIDDEN CHAMBERS

Although the water under the Templo Mayor site makes it difficult to dig there, it could also be useful. Outside air cannot reach the water, so it stays the same temperature. In constant temperatures, materials such as wood and bones are less likely to rot. This means that scientists will be able to test the wood and bone in the site to find out more about the Aztecs. By studying bones, forensic scientists can find out what the Aztecs ate and what diseases they suffered from. By testing wood, experts can find out what trees objects were made from and if they grew locally or were brought in from far away.

Experts use special equipment called **ground penetrating radar (GPR)** to discover what is under the ground. A GPR device sends energy pulses into the ground. Some of these pulses bounce back when they hit things, such as layers of brick or open spaces. The device then uses these signals to draw a map of what is under the earth. Using this technology, archaeologists have uncovered much of the hidden temple. With GPR, they hope to find secret underground rooms and tunnels that may still be hidden in Templo Mayor.

The Templo Mayor area consists of temples, platforms, and other buildings. By using GPR, experts believe they may find secret hidden chambers.

It is faster and cheaper to find an ancient site using GPR equipment such as this than it is to dig into the area. It also causes less damage.

PEOPLE OF THE PAST

Inside the Templo Mayor, there was a chilling discovery—five human skulls. Holes had been bored into the sides of the skulls. They were displayed side by side on a pole. Who did the skulls belong to?

Secrets of Skulls

Scientists can learn many things by looking at a skull. They can tell whether it belonged to a male or a female, an adult or a child. Male skulls are usually larger and thicker than female skulls, and have bigger eye sockets. Their brows and jaws also stick out more. Other clues point to how people lived. Worn-down teeth and **cavities** can be signs of a poor diet.

 This mosaic mask was made to look like the Aztec god Tezcatlipoca. Those teeth are real—forensic tests can tell us if they came from an Aztec enemy (see "Did You Know?" next page).

HOW SCIENCE SOLVED THE PAST:

COMPARING SKULLS

Forensic scientists studied the five skulls found in the Templo Mayor. They quickly saw that they belonged to three women and two men. Tests showed that the holes had been bored into the skulls after the people had died. Tests of plant remains found at the site showed that flowers were placed on the skulls. Most importantly, tests of their teeth showed that at least three of the skulls were not from Aztecs but from people who had come from far away. But who were they? Were they **migrants** or prisoners of war? Forensic tests solved some mysteries, but there are still many to be solved...

Scientists carry out tests on bones to find out if the person was male or female, their age, and the area he or she came from. This helps scientists figure out how far people traveled in early times.

THE TOWER OF SKULLS

In the Templo Mayor, investigators found a huge rack of skulls. The rack was 112 feet (34 m) tall and 40 feet (12 m) wide. On it, more than 650 skulls were strung together on long wooden poles. Each skull had small holes in it where it was threaded onto the pole, then put on display.

Hairy Stories

Who were the people on the rack? The skulls contained clues because they still had some hair and skin attached. This means the heads were probably put on the poles soon after being cut from the bodies. Scientists studied the skin and hair to find out more about these people.

HOW SCIENCE SOLVED THE PAST:

IDENTIFYING THE SKULLS

Scientists studying the Templo Mayor skulls realized that many of the victims were women and children. They carried out **DNA** tests on the skulls. DNA is a set of instructions found in every **cell** of all living things. The tests showed that most of these victims were not Aztecs but came from areas nearby. This means the victims were probably prisoners of war or captured slaves. The skull rack may have been a way for the Aztecs to show their strength and power to their enemies.

This stone wall from an Aztec temple shows carvings of the skulls of victims of sacrifice.

This crystal skull in the British Museum, England, was once believed to come from the Aztec Empire. Forensic tests showed that it contained traces of substances not found in Mexico—it was a fake, just like the one tested by the Smithsonian Institute (see left).

Scientists examine hair under powerful microscopes to find out more about the person it belonged to. The color and texture of hair can give scientists clues about where the person came from.

A BUNDLE OF BONES

Bones that are badly damaged can still tell us a lot. They show us if the person they belonged to was male or female, and how old, heavy, and tall he or she was. Damaged bones can hint at what caused the person's death, such as injury or disease. They can also show scientists if that person was murdered.

How Old?

To find out how old something is, scientists often use a technique called **carbon dating**. All living things—animals, humans, and plants—contain substances called carbons. When a living thing dies, one type of the carbon it contains starts to **decay**. Forensic scientists have tests that can measure this decay to figure out how old the human, plant, or animal remains are.

A skull contains more than 20 bones, so it can take a forensic scientist a long time to put together a smashed skull. Any piece of the skull, as well as the teeth in the jaw bone, can be tested for DNA.

HOW SCIENCE SOLVED THE PAST:

BODY OF EVIDENCE

One of the biggest Aztec finds was a burial site 16 feet (5 m) below the Templo Mayor. In it, the skeleton of a young woman was found, surrounded by 1,789 bones. These bones did not form a complete skeleton. Archaeologists have never found any other person buried like this.

Scientists tested the bones. They belong to males and females of many different ages. Some of the back and chest bones had cut marks. This means the people they belonged to may have had their hearts cut out when they were sacrificed to a god or an emperor.

Scientists want to find out where the bones came from before they were buried with the woman. They will test the soil on the bones. If it is different from the soil the bones are buried in, scientists will know the bones were dug up from elsewhere and reburied with the woman.

This statue of an eagle warrior was found at the Templo Mayor and shows the detailed costumes some fighters wore. The eagle warriors held a special place in the Aztec army.

LOST CITIES FOUND!

In 2017, researchers at Colorado State University found the lost ancient city of Angamuco. The city belonged to the Purépecha civilization. These people were enemies of the Aztecs, and lived in western Mexico. At its height in the early 1500s, Angamuco was home to more than 100,000 people. The researchers did not find Angamuco while on the ground—they found the city from the air, using a tool called **lidar**.

Seeing Through Trees

Forensic scientists can use lidar to create images of crime scenes where the ground has been disturbed or there are obstacles in the way. A lidar machine in a plane sends fast beams of **laser** light to the ground. Light is reflected back to the machine, which measures the time it takes for the light to return. Lidar can even look through the leaves of trees and find abandoned roads and building foundations on, or even below, the ground. It produces a clear 3-D map of an area, picking out high spots such as hills and low spots such as valleys. Lidar has helped uncover the wonders of the city of Angamuco, including temples, pyramids, a road system, and parks—all beneath the Mexican jungle.

DID You Know?

Archaeologists can get robots to do the exploring for them! They sent a robot into the tunnels near the Temple of the Feathered Serpent (see opposite). The **remote-controlled** robot used an **infrared** camera and a laser scanner to send back 3-D images of the tunnels. Robots help to make it easier to look into places it may be dangerous for people to go, such as deep tunnels and chambers.

It can take many months or even years to trek through thick jungle in the search for hidden ancient cities. An easier and quicker way to explore is from above, using aircraft and lidar technology.

Beneath the Temple of the Feathered Serpent (see below) archaeologists found skulls surrounded by human jaws. Forensic scientists will use DNA tests on the skulls and teeth to find out where the people came from, how they lived, and if they were from the same family.

HOW SCIENCE SOLVED THE PAST:

UNDERGROUND SECRETS REVEALED

In 2003, after a heavy rainstorm, a huge hole appeared near the Temple of the Feathered Serpent, in the ancient city of Teotihuacan. Experts believed it led to a series of secret tunnels and chambers dating from Aztec times. Before archaeologists could go down into the tunnels, they had to map the area using the latest forensic science technology. Forensic scientists used GPR to find out how many tunnels were below, and how long they were. They also uncovered secret chambers. It took nearly a year to complete a **digital** map of the site.

Lidar scanners, such as this one, use a laser beam to measure the distance between it and solid objects underground, such as a wall or floor.

RIVERS OF DANGER

The city of Teotihuacan is nearly 1,800 years old—much older than the Aztecs. But it became an important religious center for the Aztecs, who gave the city its name, meaning "city of the gods." Teotihuacan is surrounded by tunnels. Archaeologists dug out nearly 1,000 tons (907 metric tons) of soil from the tunnels, preserving artifacts they found. Then, at the end of one tunnel, 55 feet (17 m) underground, they found something else: pools of **mercury**.

Poisonous Work

To work in the tunnels, the scientists had to take safety precautions. Mercury is highly poisonous. Mercury poisoning can lead to breathing difficulties and, if enough of it builds up in the body, death.

DID You Know?

When archaeologists finally started exploring the end of the tunnels, they found large collections of surrounding treasures and jewels, possible teeth, and bones from the city. For this reason, scientists believe that it may be a royal burial site for local rulers. The mercury is one of many clues that lead scientists to believe the tomb is near. If mercury is found underground, there may be something else underground the archaeologists have yet to find.

When scientists find water in a cave, they may test it to make sure it does not contain a poisonous material such as mercury.

Forensic scientists working with the mercury had to wear goggles and special clothing to protect their skin and eyes. They had to wear masks to keep them from breathing in harmful **vapor**. After work, all their clothing had to be collected and washed by special teams trained in working with dangerous materials.

HOW SCIENCE SOLVED THE PAST:

THE TUNNEL OF STARS

Forensic scientists test unknown substances to identify them and see if they are **toxic** or dangerous. They test substances at a crime scene to see what chemicals, such as drugs or poisons, they might contain.

One tunnel discovered by archaeologists had a ceiling that glittered like the night sky. Forensic scientists tested powder samples from the tunnel roof. They think the powder contains metals called pyrite and magnetite. These metals reflect light and look like twinkling stars. Researchers believe that these metals are not found in this region. This means that the Aztecs brought metals from somewhere else and used them to paint the tunnel ceiling.

The Aztecs believed mirror-like surfaces were doors into other worlds. Shiny pyrite metal, known as "fool's gold," was used to create mirrors in the tunnels.

Beneath the Temple of the Feathered Serpent, scientists are exploring hidden tunnels that have been sealed for hundreds of years.

A TURKEY DINNER?

The Aztecs were great farmers. They grew enough food to feed hundreds of thousands of people. We know the Aztecs grew and ate a lot of corn, and that they ate meat. Two animals they especially liked to eat were turkeys—and hairless dogs!

Looking for Leftovers

Forensic scientists can find out what ancient people ate by studying food remains, cooking pots, and the soil from places where food was cooked. To test soil, they use a technique called **flotation**. In a flotation test, soil is put on a **mesh**. This is a wire cloth with many tiny holes. Water is then gently bubbled up through the soil. Lighter items in the soil, such as seeds, float to the top. Heavier materials, such as pieces of bone, stay on the mesh. Scientists can then study the pieces of bone to find out what animal they came from. They can examine the seeds under a microscope to find out what crop they belong to. This information tells scientists what animals the Aztecs ate and what crops they grew.

Scientists examine food cells such as these under a microscope to help them figure out what the Aztecs ate or fed to their animals.

This painting, made by an Aztec artist, shows Aztec women preparing turkey for a feast.

AZTEC TURKEY FARMS

Tests on turkey bones found in temples and human graves suggest the turkeys were fed crops grown by the Aztecs. This information shows that the turkeys were raised on farms rather than caught in the wild. It proves that turkeys were very important to the Aztecs—some ancient pictures even show the Aztecs worshiping turkeys as gods!

« Forensic tests on the remains of Aztec turkeys show that, in Aztec times, the birds would have been much smaller, with less meat on them than today's plump turkeys.

DID You Know?

The Thanksgiving turkey started life with the Aztecs. Spanish invaders took Aztec turkeys from Mexico back to Spain. There they farmed them, and traded them with the rest of Europe. When people from Europe went to live in the "New World" of America, they took turkeys with them. Just think—the turkey you eat at Thanksgiving is the **descendent** of an Aztec turkey!

MUMMY MYSTERY

In 1999, archaeologists discovered the bodies of three **Inca** children near the top of a mountain in Argentina, in South America. The children had lived at the same time as the Aztecs, more than 500 years ago. The cold, dry mountain air had preserved the children's bodies. In fact, their clothes, skin, and hair were so well preserved that the children looked as though they had just fallen asleep. We call bodies that are very well preserved "mummies."

The Secrets of the Mummy's Hair

Chemical tests on hair and DNA tests showed that one of the mummies was a 13-year-old girl. Tests on her skin and bones showed that the girl had begun to eat a lot of meat before she died. This told scientists that she had become an important person, because only wealthy Incas could afford to eat a lot of meat. Tests on her hair showed that in the last six months of her life, the girl had drunk a lot of alcohol, and that she was left out on the cold mountain and died of exposure. Scientists also found that the girl was drugged.

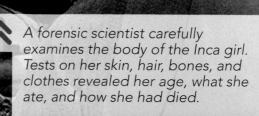

A forensic scientist carefully examines the body of the Inca girl. Tests on her skin, hair, bones, and clothes revealed her age, what she ate, and how she had died.

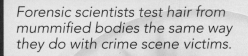

Forensic scientists test hair from mummified bodies the same way they do with crime scene victims.

HOW SCIENCE SOLVED THE PAST:

THE MYSTERIOUS BOY

At a different site in Argentina, another possible sacrifice victim was found—a young boy. But who was he? To find out, scientists took DNA samples from his lungs. Different types of DNA are passed from both parents to their child, and these create a special DNA group that only that child has. The results from the boy showed that his mother, or her **ancestors**, were not from Argentina but had come from Peru. This is a country nearly 1,000 miles (1,610 km) to the north of Argentina. This shows that people in Aztec times traveled very long distances.

The rich and powerful in ancient times were buried with items they might need in the next life. Tests can find out what materials were used to make the objects and how they were made. All this helps experts build up a clearer picture of ancient civilizations.

END OF THE EMPIRE

Around 5 to 15 million Aztecs died during an **epidemic** that took place after the Spanish arrived in Mexico in the 1500s. Experts believed the Spanish had brought a disease with them—possibly measles, smallpox, or the flu.

Ancient Bugs

To find out more about the mysterious disease, in 2000, scientists tested the teeth of 29 Aztecs who had died at the time of the epidemic. They used a new DNA test that could trace the **bacteria** and **viruses** that cause different types of illnesses. They hoped this test would show them exactly what type of illness had wiped out the Aztecs.

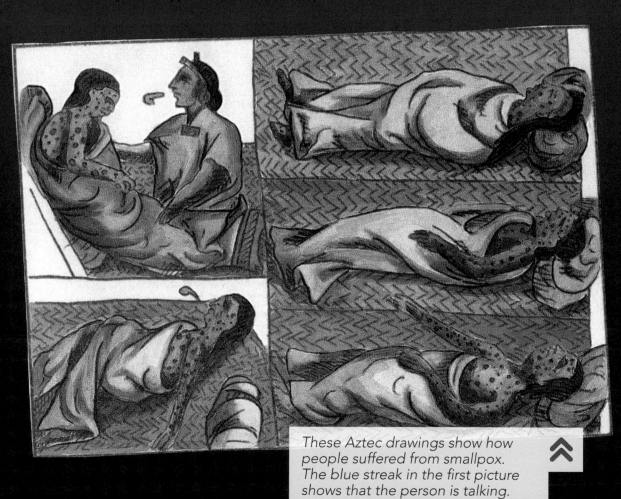

These Aztec drawings show how people suffered from smallpox. The blue streak in the first picture shows that the person is talking.

The new test found DNA
belonging to salmonella, a
type of bacteria sometimes
found in food that can
make people very sick.
The sick Aztecs would
have gotten red spots
on the skin, vomited,
bled from the nose,
and coughed up blood.
DNA tests on Aztecs
who had died before the
Spanish invaded showed
no signs of salmonella.
The particular type of
salmonella the scientists
found is now very rare, but
in Aztec times it would have
caused a deadly sickness.

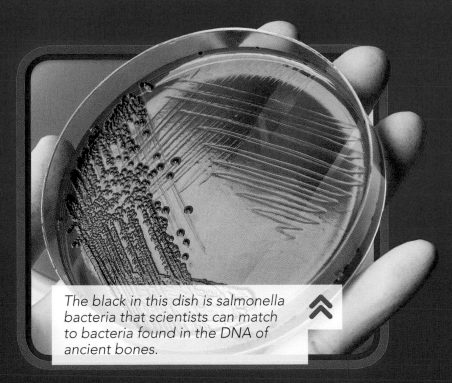

*The black in this dish is salmonella
bacteria that scientists can match
to bacteria found in the DNA of
ancient bones.*

Scientists think the Spanish were used
to the salmonella bacteria and could
carry it without getting sick. The Aztecs
had never faced the bacteria before, and
their **immune systems** had no defense
against it, so it killed them very quickly.

HOW SCIENCE SOLVED THE PAST:
TESTING TEETH

DNA testing on a Norwegian woman
who died in 1200 C.E. showed she was
carrying the same type of salmonella
that killed the Aztecs. This means
the bacteria had been in Europe
300 years before it appeared in the
Aztec Empire. This forensic discovery
could be further evidence that the
bacteria that killed the Aztecs was
brought over to Mexico by
the Spanish.

DID
You Know?

Teeth are a good source when looking
for DNA because they last longer than
skin or hair. In 2018, scientists in Germany
tested 24 bodies taken from a burial
ground in Teposcolula-Yucundaa in
southern Mexico. DNA samples taken
from the teeth of these bodies identified
not only the human they came from,
but also any viruses and bacteria
those people may have had.

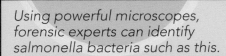

*Using powerful microscopes,
forensic experts can identify
salmonella bacteria such as this.*

FORENSIC FUTURE

We are learning more about the Aztecs every day, but there is still much to discover. For example, no one has yet found a tomb of an Aztec king. As technology advances, **drones** and satellites will help scientists search for hidden tombs and temples deep within the thick, steamy jungle of Mexico. Robots will squeeze into places human scientists cannot go. What might they find?

When they do find hidden sites in the future, scientists will be able to date artifacts more accurately than they can today. DNA tests on human remains will reveal clues about where the Aztecs came from and the life they lived. Advances in technology are finding clues to the past that we never knew existed, and providing a fascinating gateway to ancient lives. What might forensic science uncover in the future? Our picture of life in Aztec times is becoming clearer with every tiny piece of the puzzle that is discovered and pieced together.

DID
You Know?

The Aztecs were mostly within the West until the quirate won thriv ade moving flelds of 1 set way or ther. The city of Tenochtitlan was built on water. So the Aztecs there used boats to carry supplies to and from the city. But how did people in the rest of the empire transport supplies without using wheels? Scientists hope future forensics will reveal answers to this mystery.

Aztec emperors wore colorful feather headdresses such as this. The feathers can be tested to find out what type of birds they came from.

CAN FORENSICS SOLVE...?

Here are two of the great still-unsolved mysteries about the ancient Aztecs. Forensic scientists are using forensic footprints to try to solve these mysteries, too!

Mystery Tree

Another puzzling discovery at the Templo Mayor was an old tree trunk. The tree is thought to be somehow involved in sacrifices. The tree trunk was found stuck in a round base made of rock from a volcano. Forensic tests on the tree could tell scientists where the tree came from and what sort of tree it is. Chemical tests might also find traces of blood on it. This would confirm that it was an important part of Aztec sacrifices.

The Cracked Skulls

When archaeologists discovered the Templo Mayor, they found 50 skulls at a stone used for sacrifices. Five skulls were buried under the stone. Holes in the skulls mean that at one time they were hung on a skull rack. Scientists say the other 45 skulls appear to have just been thrown on top of the stone. This has puzzled historians and scientists. It does not fit in with the way Aztec sacrifices have been reported from ancient writings, or with the results of forensic testing on other sacrificial sites.

If the skulls were on a rack, why were they taken off and buried? Why were five skulls buried and the others left on top? Scientists believe the skulls on top may have been dug up from other sites and brought to this one, but they do not know why. Forensic tests on soil could help scientists figure out if the other skulls all came from different sites. Tests on the skulls could give scientists clues about who the sacrificed people were. Could they have been local people, slaves, or even prisoners of war?

Tests on skulls from the Templo Mayor may solve mysteries about how the Aztecs sacrificed people.

GLOSSARY

Please note: Some **bold-faced** words are defined where they appear in the book.

ancestors Relatives who died long ago

anthropologists Experts who study who ancient people were, how they lived, and where they came from

archaeologists Experts who study where ancient people lived and the things they left behind

bacteria Tiny living things that can cause disease

carbon dating A way to find out the age of an object by measuring the amount of a type of carbon atom that changes at a known rate over a period of time

cavities Holes in teeth caused by decay

cell The smallest working piece of an organism

ceramic A kind of pottery made from clay that has been heated to a very high temperature

civilization A settled and stable community in which people live together peacefully and use systems such as writing to communicate

crystal A clear, hard substance used in making jewelry

decay To rot and break down

descendent Someone who is related to a person or group of people who lived

digital

forensic science The use of scientific methods and techniques to find clues about crimes or the past

foundations Solid structures that support a building from underneath

immune systems The parts of the body that fight off diseases and illnesses

Inca An ancient civilization that existed at the same time as the Aztecs in South America

infrared A type of light that feels warm but cannot be seen

laser A very narrow, highly concentrated beam of light

Maya An ancient civilization that existed in Mexico and parts of Central America before the Aztecs

mercury A silvery, poisonous liquid metal

microscopes Devices used to see objects that are too small to be seen by the naked eye

migrants People who voluntarily leave their home country to live in another country

mosaic A kind of decoration in which small pieces of glass or stone are stuck to a surface

mythical Existing only in the imagination

nomads People who have no fixed home but instead move from place to place

preserve To make sure something stays the same

pyramids Large buildings with a square base

remains

scanning electron microscope A microscope that scans something using a beam of electrons, and creates an image based on how the electrons are reflected back at the scanner

sites Places where something is or has been

techniques Methods of doing particular tasks

temples Buildings where people worship a god or gods

three-dimensional (3-D) Having or appearing to have length, width, and depth

Toltecs An ancient civilization that existed in Mexico before the Aztecs

toxic Harmful to living things

vapor An almost invisible steam that rises from a substance

viruses Tiny organisms that cause disease

LEARNING MORE

Books

Deem, James M. *Faces from the Past: Forgotten People of North America*. HMH Books for Young Readers, 2012.

Green, Jen, Fiona MacDonald, Philip Steele, and Michael Stotter. *Encyclopedia of the Ancient Americas: The Everyday Life of America's Native Peoples*. Southwater, 2018.

Murray, Laura K. *Exploring the Aztec Empire*. 12-Story Library, 2018.

Stoltman, Joan. *The Rise and Fall of the Aztec Empire (World History)*. Lucent Books, 2018.

Websites

www.aztec-history.com
A site dedicated to the history of the Aztecs, full of articles, timelines, and descriptions of their life and culture.

http://aztecs.mrdonn.org
Learn about the life and the history of the Aztecs, as well as other important civilizations in history, through fun articles.

www.dkfindout.com/us/history/aztecs
Discover more about the Aztecs, from their capital to their gods.

https://kids.kiddle.co/world-history/aztecs
Games and quizzes and visual features help you discover more about the society and culture of the Aztecs, along with other historical events.

INDEX

Angamuco 18
anthropologists 5
archaeologists 5, 6, 8, 9, 10, 11,
   17, 18, 19, 20, 21, 29
artwork 7, 10, 12, 14, 16, 17, 22,
   25, 26
Aztlán 4

bacteria and viruses 26–27
ball game court 8, 9
blood 5, 9, 27, 29
bones 5, 8, 9, 10, 11, 12, 13, 16,
   17, 19, 20, 22, 23, 24, 27

cacao beans 7
carbon dating 16, 17
children 5, 14, 24
chocolate 7
crime scenes 5, 6, 18, 21, 25
crystal skulls 15

digital maps 19
DNA testing 14, 17, 20, 24, 25,
   26, 27, 28
dogs 9, 22

eagle warrior 17

hair 14–15, 24, 25, 27
headdresses 28

isotopes 12, 13, 23

Lake Texcoco 4
lidar 18, 19

magnetite 21
masks 7, 12, 13
Maya 17
meats 12, 22, 23, 24
mercury 20
Mexico City 5, 8, 10, 17
microscopes 6, 15, 22, 27
Moctezuma II 4
mosaics 7, 12
moving things 28
mummies 24–25

poisonous substances 20–21
preserving artifacts 6, 10, 20
Purépecha civilization 18
pyramids 4, 18
corn 21

section

teeth 5, 9, 12, 13, 19, 20, 27
Temple of the Feathered Serpent
   18, 19, 21
temples 4, 11, 13, 18, 19, 21, 28
Templo Mayor 10–11, 12, 13, 14,
   17, 29
Tenochtitlan 4, 8, 9, 13, 28
Teotihuacan 19, 20
Teposcolula-Yucundaa 27
Tezcatlipoca 12
three-dimensional (3-D) models 6
Toltecs 17
tombs 5, 10, 28
tunnels 11, 18, 19, 20, 21
turkeys 22, 23

wood 10, 11, 29

About the Author

James Bow is the author of more than 60 non-fiction books for children and young
adults. He has a bachelor's degree in Environmental Sciences, and sometimes
conducts forensic investigations of his children's messy rooms.